THE HERO AND THE GIRL NEXT DOOR

The Hero and the Girl Next Door

SOPHIE HANNAH

CARCANET

To my parents with love

Acknowledgements

Some of these poems have previously appeared in *The Arcadian, As Girls Could Boast, Envoi, The Forward Book of Poetry 1994, The Frogmore Papers, Headlock, Lancaster Litfest Anthology 1993, The North, Pen & Keyboard, PN Review, Poetry London Newsletter, Poetry Nottingham, Poetry Review, The Rialto, Scratch, Slow Dancer, The Spectator, Spectrum, Staple, Tandem, Terrible Work, The Times Saturday Review, TOPS, Vision On '92*; and also in *Early Bird Blues* (Smith/Doorstop, 1993), *Second Helping of Your Heart* (Frogmore Press, 1994), and *New Poetries* (Carcanet, 1994).

First published in 1995 by
Carcanet Press Limited
402-406 Corn Exchange Buildings
Manchester M4 3BY

A CIP catalogue record for this book
is available from the British Library.
ISBN 1 85754 113 8

The publisher acknowledges financial assistance
from the Arts Council of England

Set in 10pt Palatino by Bryan Williamson, Frome
Printed and bound in England by SRP Ltd, Exeter

Contents

Soft Companion

for Lawrence Gough

He sat in the under-heated flat, alone,
Usefully passing time (he thought by choice),
Not missing anything, until the phone
Brought him the soft companion of your voice,

And then he looked around himself and saw
The scraps of clothing on the floor, in shreds,
And felt his keys hang heavy in the door.
He thought of powdered milk and single beds.

Unsure of him, you said, 'It's only me,'
Meaning not quite enough, but you were right:
Yours was the only face he hoped to see
And only you remembered him tonight.

Summary of a Western

We see a dusty desert scene and that's
The way the film begins. Some men in hats
Deliver gritty lines. They all wear braces.
They're cool and tough. They hate the darker races
Who paint peculiar stripes across their faces.

Goodies meet baddies, mostly in corrals.
Cowboys ignore or patronise their gals.
We see a gun twirl in a macho hand.
Who's killing whom we don't quite understand –
There's always some vague reference to the land.

Women in aprons have to be protected.
Stagecoaches fall. New sheriffs are elected.
The cast consists primarily of horses –
They gallop to the ending, which of course is
A happy one, where nobody divorces.

Symptoms

Although you have given me a stomach upset,
weak knees, a lurching heart, a fuzzy brain,
a high-pitched laugh, a monumental phone bill,
a feeling of unworthiness, sharp pain
when you are somewhere else, a guilty conscience,
a longing, and a dread of what's in store,
a pulse rate for the *Guinness Book of Records* –
life now is better than it was before.

Although you have given me a raging temper,
insomnia, a rising sense of panic,
a hopeless challenge, bouts of introspection,
raw, bitten nails, a voice that's strangely manic,
a selfish streak, a fear of isolation,
a silly smile, lips that are chapped and sore,
a running joke, a risk, an inspiration –
life now is better than it was before.

Although you have given me a premonition,
chattering teeth, a goal, a lot to lose,
a granted wish, mixed motives, superstitions,
hang-ups and headaches, fear of awful news,
a bubble in my throat, a dare to swallow,
a crack of light under a closing door,
the crude, fantastic prospect of forever –
life now is better than it was before.

The Affair

The lamp post bends his head. His face is red
above the frozen fringes of the street.
Dishevelled night is climbing into bed.
She strokes the waking clock, then steals the sheet.

Something disturbs the symmetry of hedges;
a recent scandal seeping through the grass.
The breathing curtains lose their heavy edges,
touched by the light that settles on the glass.

A small dog kicks the pavement into stretching.
The postbox mouth hangs open for receiving.
I almost hear a taxi driver fetching
your suitcase. Very soon you will be leaving.

Six Sonnets

WHEN I AM FAMOUS

When I am famous, in the years to come,
I know how keen you'll be to share the glory;
When journalists whip out a hefty sum
Before your nose, to make you sell our story,
You'll have no qualms. I, therefore, will expect
Full details of our sex life in *The Sun*.
I will not sue you, nor will I object
In any way – I'll treat it as good fun.
Make sure to give them all the dirty bits.
The truth gets dull – why not throw in some lies,
Some strange inventions? Say I've got three tits
Or four. Meanwhile, I've got a nice surprise
In store for you – I'll make you tremble yet:
I know about your flower-pressing set.

WRONG AGAIN

I did the right thing once (may God reward me);
Restrained myself. I took a moral stance.
Virtue, I found, was not my thing – it bored me
Rigid, and I would like another chance
To earn myself a wicked reputation
Equal to yours. I'll match you sin for sin.
Lies, promiscuity, inebriation –
It all sounds lovely. When can we begin?
I used to be afraid of rumours spreading.
You made my fear seem fussy, immature.
Here's my new motto, then: just change the bedding
And carry on exactly as before.
A single, happy night beneath your quilt
Is all I want. I'll risk post-coital guilt.

THE PHILANDERER'S ANSAPHONE MESSAGE

I'm not at home to take your call. Bad luck,
But leave your number and I'll be in touch.
You'll hear from me next time I want a fuck,
(My love, my darling). Thank you very much.
Please leave your name – I'll add it to my list,
That way I won't forget. One does lose track...
But I can guarantee that when I'm pissed
I shall be keen to get you in the sack.
I knew this ansaphone would come in handy –
Voice after female voice I've got recorded.
I play the tape back when I'm feeling randy
And one by one my ladies are rewarded.
My system works supremely well, I've found.
Wait by the phone until your turn comes round.

A SHALLOW END

It's not a present. Call it a reward.
The pool is yours. I'll charge you for the water.
A shallow end, perhaps, you could afford.
    I would like a cut-price coffin to bury my daughter.

They give you rice or chips with every meal.
Look, two cremations for the price of one!
A car drives past without a single wheel.
    I would like a second-hand coffin to bury my son.

My ornaments were sad to see me go.
I must remind them that we still vote Labour.
Return the plum tomato that you owe.
    I would like a hole in the garden to bury my neighbour.

But to go to Rome and not speak a word of Latin!
    I would like a very cheap coffin to bury my cat in.

ONE-TRACK MIND

Why does she take unnecessary trips?
She lives just opposite a row of shops.
She went to Crewe to buy a bag of chips.
She went to Birmingham to buy lamb chops.

She has no time for aeroplanes or boats.
She cannot get enough of British Rail.
She went to Liverpool for Quaker Oats
Then Halifax to buy the *Daily Mail*.

She went to Chester for a pair of tights.
Every weekend she's up and down some track.
She went to York for twenty Marlboro Lights.
She went to Stalybridge and came straight back.

Once, on her way to Hull for cottage cheese,
She saw him. All he said was *Tickets, please*.

A FAIRLY UNIVERSAL SET

Whoever cleans your windows once a week,
Whoever stuffs your letters through the door,
Whoever you'd get in to fix a leak –
I resent all of these and plenty more.

Men on the bus and women in the street,
Religious nuts who ring your bell at dawn,
Any chiropodist who's touched your feet,
Canvassers, tramps, whoever mows your lawn,

Your colleagues, friends, acquaintances (both sexes),
People with whom you've shared a cigarette,
Your enemies, and, most of all, your exes,
Everyone you have ever seen or met,

Voices you might from time to time have heard,
The speaking clock. Jealous is not the word.

Before Sherratt & Hughes
Became Waterstone's

Romantic entanglements often occur
In a pub or a railway station,
But being a writer I tend to prefer
A suitably bookish location.

I've never liked nightclubs, nor am I the sort
To go for a snog in the loos.
By far the most interesting place to cavort
Is the ground floor of Sherratt & Hughes.

I've seen a few customers looking dismayed,
Too British to voice their objection,
But how can I help it? I like to get laid
Just in front of the poetry section.

Most people prefer a luxurious setting –
A Mediterranean cruise,
But to my mind, the place most conducive to petting
Is the ground floor of Sherratt & Hughes.

All it takes is one glimpse of a gold-lettered spine
On those lovingly organised shelves
And a human encounter seems almost divine –
Not just sex, but a merging of selves.

I have never been someone who strictly adheres
To what's proper – I do as I choose.
(I go down very well with the male cashiers
On the ground floor of Sherratt & Hughes.)

Two-Headed Dog Street

Walking down two-headed dog street on my
way to work is such an upsetting
experience that I prefer to stay at home.

I prefer to stay at home, but I
have trouble conveying this to my
boss, who is lucky enough to have never
needed to walk down two-headed dog street.

Two-headed dog street is the only route to
everywhere I want to go, which is why I
usually stay inside and rarely
dare to open my kitchen window.

From my kitchen window there's a very good view
of two-headed dog street, where old dustbin
bags grow into people, and where
handbags are liable to have nervous breakdowns.

Nervous breakdowns frequently occur on
two-headed dog street, and even I, who
do not live there, have been known to
participate from time to time.

From time to time I am forced to walk
down two-headed dog street, and the only way
to reach the other end is to
pretend that I am a two-headed dog.

The Gift

I am saving my money
to buy you a raw potato.

I will scrub it with my nailbrush
and bathe it in my basin.

I will cut out your initials
from its smooth, brown jacket.

I will gift-wrap it in pink paper
and tie it with pink ribbons.

I will place it in a shoe-box
on a bed of tissue paper.

I will deliver it to your doorstep,
wearing pink shoes.

You will stare at it crossly at first,
as if it were a baby.

You will take it inside quickly
to stop the neighbours staring.

You will not know where to put it.
You will be afraid to hold it.

You will hide it in your bedroom
to protect it from stray glances.

It will live in the furthest corner
forever, and embarrass you.

Mad Queen Hospital for Electrifying the Heart*

Welcome. My cocoa-buttered hands
Built these five rooms, undid this face,
Untangled all that once made sense.
The hall stands bare for compliments,
For chaos – an escape from peace.
So far so good. I'm in demand.

They bring their lives like powdered soup
For me to stir, and sniff, and drink;
The healing process, cruel to be
As cruel as they have been to me.
I am the one they have to thank.
I fill their rooms with scented soap.

Five at a time. The royal need
To charge their hearts, to be in charge,
Is almost physical, a craving.
I crave to save those not worth saving.
A mind once small that swells too large
Is happy as a hand grenade.

After explosion, fully trained,
Their feet leave scars on bedroom rugs,
Their frenzy stains the corridors.
Clutching their hearts, expensive sores,
They pay the bill. I bleach the rags,
The ash, the lives they leave behind.

Doors beckon shut. My vacant palace,
Drooling, awaits the next arrivals.
Five relentless rooms to let
And nobody has caught me yet.
It's pure; a matter of survival,
No grudges held, no taint of malice.

* The title of this poem is an extract from a poem called
'Telephone Directory' by Harry Crosby.

17

Minding his Boots

He likes to walk around barefoot
while I mind his boots – the only part
of him which can stand still.

Pieces of broken glass and stones
don't seem to cut; his soles are tough,
dark like leather, skin socks.

Here is the trail of flat-crushed daisies
his going left behind, small white
and yellow crumbs in grass.

He is unreachable, framed
in an accidental afternoon
that lingers, hungry for souvenirs.

These boots which he leaves in my care
will belong to me longer than he will belong
to any earth, any air.

Something Coming

The pavement shone with news of something coming,
or just with rain. She took it as a warning,
identical to last time – first the humming,
then thunder, then his letter in the morning.

She did her best to see some sort of sense
in all these things, to make them fit together.
At the same time she laughed at the pretence
that love could be connected with the weather,

which can't be true, or life would be too frightening
to live. Next time she swore she'd go to bed
and not stay up to study trends of lightning
and wonder what, if anything, they said.

A Day Too Late

You meet a man. You're looking for a hero,
Which you pretend he is. A day too late
You realise his sex appeal is zero
And you begin to dread the second date.

You'd love to stand him up but he's too clever –
He knows by heart your work and home address.
Last night he said he'd stay with you forever.
You fear he might have meant it. What a mess!

That's when you start regretting his existence.
It's all his fault. You hate him with a passion.
You hate his love, his kindness, his persistence.
He's too intense. His clothes are out of fashion.

Shortly you reach the stage of desperation.
At first you thought about behaving well
And giving him an honest explanation.
Now all you want to say is 'Go to Hell',

And even that seems just a touch too gentle.
Deep down, the thing that makes you want to weep
Is knowing that you once felt sentimental
About this wholly unattractive creep.

Trainers All Turn Grey

(after Robert Frost's 'Nothing Gold Can Stay')

You buy your trainers new.
They cost a bob or two.
At first they're clean and white,
The laces thick and tight.
Then they must touch the ground –
(You have to walk around).
You learn to your dismay
Trainers all turn grey.

Another Filling

My sister knows my name and nothing else.
My mother knows my shoe size.
My father knows what kind of books I read.

My friends know where I drink.
My husband knows the colour of my hair.
My children know my rules.

My dentist knows I need another filling.
My boss knows I work late.
My cat knows that I'll share a turkey sandwich.

I know what makes me laugh.
I laugh at what they don't know.
They don't know very much about my dentist.

Introducing Vanity

A powder compact for a face,
White feet whose soles avoid the ground
But tread on lace,
Making a soft, material sound
In halls
Where heavy mirrors line the walls.

Bone china skin, pale jasmine breath;
In every sense an ornament.
Some pretty death
Will face her in the tournament.
A ghost,
She'll be more visible than most.

Her pointed features will impress
Insistent pouts upon the air.
She'll overdress
And wrap thick scarves around her hair;
Concealed
So that her shape might be revealed.

Stars will throw glitter on her jewels.
Inventor of the heart-shaped locket,
She collects fools
To put in her embroidered pocket.
She asks
For no-one to remove the masks.

Second Helping of Your Heart

1

I can't remember saying that I wanted this,
But these things happen. (Enter other platitudes.)
I was your midnight scrap. You left your haunted kiss
On my cold lips, without once changing attitudes.

A woman packs a suitcase in the south.
Calf-muscles ache. She may be feeling old tonight,
Or be in bed. Her understudy's mouth
Treats dirty fag-ends like small bars of gold tonight.

I can't remember mixing the ingredients.
Did I or did I not play any part in this?
(Enter a childhood training in obedience.)
Is there a second helping of your heart in this?

The inefficiency of most removal men
Is something that you cannot bear to think about.
Why I should bother chasing your approval when
I disapprove is something I must drink about.

Here, under chilly light and wooden beams,
My thumbnail is too long. It's like a talon.
Here is your parting gift: disruptive dreams
From four till seven. (Enter Woody Allen.)

2

If we examine ratios of power, praise
Becomes a farce. I start to doubt its origin
And its sincerity. Your leaning tower ways
Make bowls of women, fit for slopping porridge in.

Do I have any choice but to give way to you,
Here, in this echo-box? The shadows creep outside.
The sober cynic in me wants to say to you,
'Why bother with me, dear, when there are sheep outside?'

But you're too genuine, too off-the-cuff to be
Kept at a distance, treated with disparagement.
Let us not mention what you're old enough to be
Or that you're still not quite sure what your marriage meant.

So. Do you really think my work is saleable?
And will your confidence in me deflate a bit
If I declare my body unavailable,
All heavy, disbelieving five foot eight of it?

(Enter a fear of alcohol-dependency,
Tomorrow morning, what the hell I'll say to you.)
I can't risk heights and depths. I have a tendency
To step around such things. And so good day to you.

For the Following Reasons

Because strands of wool do not trail
from the sleeves of my jumper.

Because I would never stop reading a book
three pages before the end.

Because I brush teeth not tooth.

Because I wait for the aeroplane
to land before stepping outside.

Because I like to do things properly.

Because I like people to know what I mean
and do not stop talking or writing until they do.

Because I don't waste time on jigsaws
with only one piece,

or send letters without my signature,

or eat lunch without digesting it,

or brush all the hair to the left of my head,
ignoring what grows on the right.

Because I can only tolerate moments
if they are firmly lodged in hours.

Because I am orderly and extrapolate
neat patterns from the most uncertain things

you will be hearing from me again.

Two Rondels

THE END OF LOVE

The end of love should be a big event.
It should involve the hiring of a hall.
Why the hell not? It happens to us all.
Why should it pass without acknowledgement?

Suits should be dry-cleaned, invitations sent.
Whatever form it takes – a tiff, a brawl –
The end of love should be a big event.
It should involve the hiring of a hall.

Better than the unquestioning descent
Into the trap of silence, than the crawl
From visible to hidden, door to wall.

Get the announcements made, the money spent.
The end of love should be a big event.
It should involve the hiring of a hall.

MORE TROUBLE THAN FUN

We cannot undo what we've done
But we don't have to do any more.
What on earth are we doing it for
If it's so much more trouble than fun?

If you want, I can act like a nun.
I'll be meek and incredibly pure.
We cannot undo what we've done
But we don't have to do any more.

Just remember that you were the one
Who complained that your life was a bore.
Now you suddenly feel insecure.

Will it help if you panic and run?
We cannot undo what we've done
But we don't have to do any more.

Call Yourself a Poet

I called myself an architect,
Designed a huge sky-scraper.
How powerful it looked, erect
Upon my piece of paper.
Presto! The housing problem solved!
(I'd had no formal training.)
My pride and joy collapsed, dissolved,
The day it started raining.

I gave up architecture then
And called myself a vet.
My failure, time and time again,
To save a well-loved pet
Annoyed the RSPCA.
They went around campaigning
And I was forced to move away.
(I'd had no formal training.)

My next career was plumbing.
Easy enough, you'd think,
But I spent hours drumming
My fingers on the sink,
Scared to approach the toilet.
All blockages remained,
Which somehow seemed to spoil it.
(Perhaps I should have trained.)

I didn't dare to drive a van
So I became a poet.
I couldn't rhyme, make sense or scan
Yet no-one seemed to know it.
I knew that I had hit upon
My ultimate vocation
The day I met an Oxford don
Who praised my innovation.

Only last week I found myself
The subject of a lecture,
My book on some professor's shelf.
So who needs architecture,
Knowledge of water pipes? What fools
Dabble in surgery?
Oh, how restrictive! All those rules!
While verse, my friends, is free.

Amusing Myself

Here is the form I should have signed,
The book I should be reading.
Every attempt is undermined
By thoughts of you, stampeding.
I try to still them; am resigned
To not succeeding.

Here is the card I would have sent,
The fruit I would be peeling
If every second wasn't spent
On you, but while each feeling
Goes where its predecessor went
There'll be no healing.

Here are the words I'm scared to use.
You wouldn't catch me saying
This to your face, though I amuse
Myself and God by praying
That you'll be back; next time confuse
Me more by staying.

Differences

Not everyone who wears a hat
Is copying the Queen.
Not everything that's large and flat
Thinks it's a movie screen.
If every time I dress in blue
I imitate the sea,
It makes no difference what I do –
Nothing is down to me.

Not every dim, electric light
Would like to be the sun.
A water pistol doesn't quite
Mimic a loaded gun.
I do my best, I do my worst
With my specific heart –
God and the Devil got there first;
They had an early start.

Tomatoes can be round and red
Yet be distinct from Mars.
Not all the things above my head
Can be described as stars.
The world had better learn what's what
(If it remotely cares) –
A ladder is a ladder, not
A failed attempt at stairs.

The Answer

Why do you give the impression that you'd rather
not be loved? You almost tell people not to bother.
Why are you neither one thing nor the other?

Why do you fluctuate between ticks and crosses,
alternate between flippancy and neurosis?
Won't you confirm or contradict my guesses?

What is it that you do, by simply sitting
with your elbows raised, that makes me sick of waiting?
Why is your absence tantamount to cheating?

I know you're real, which means you must pay taxes,
catch colds and snore. I know you know what sex is.
Still, there is something in you that never mixes,

something that smells like the air in silver boxes.

It makes me suddenly afraid of asking,
suddenly sure of all the things I'm risking.

No Competition

I am in favour of a law being passed,
forbidding, to everyone but you, the use
of the word *whirlwind*.

I am in favour, also, of a law
being passed, restricting your vocabulary
to *whirlwind* only.

Here is how it would be in practical terms:
you, in the centre of a circular room,
unresentful, eyes closed, mouth open, and the word
whirlwind filling the room again and again.

Silence apart from this. No competition
from inferior words. Listeners on cushions
kissing the polished floor.

Friends Again

Let's sort this out. Make no more cherry
scones for the man that stole my jewels
and I'll stop spitting in your sherry.
Both of us have been fools.

Here, you can have my rope and pins
if you give up your hooks and nails
and we'll agree to wear wide grins
for subsequent betrayals.

Even a bond as firm as this
friendship cannot withstand attacks
if they are too direct; let's hiss
behind each other's backs.

In future, when I tread thick soil
into your house, I'll hide my feet,
and if you have to be disloyal
please try to be discreet.

The Mystery of the Missing

Think carefully. You sat down on a bench
and turned the pages of a small green book.
You were about to meet your friends for lunch.

> I turned the pages but I didn't look.
> It felt as if the bench was in mid-air.
> Whatever held me wouldn't put me back.

What happened next? You must have gone somewhere.
The wind was blowing hair across your face.
Perhaps you went inside and lit a fire.

> But people looked for me and found no trace
> inside or out. I saw the things they feared
> in the green book before I lost my place.

Surely they weren't afraid you'd disappeared?
Did they suspect you might have come to harm?
You could have reassured them with a word.

> I wanted to, but every word that came
> threatened to burn my mouth. I also knew
> that soon it would be over, I'd be home.

The sky closed in. You say you shrank, then grew,
then everything came back to you with ease.
You sat quite still, deciding what to do.

> Huge purple bruises covered both my knees
> But no-one acted like I'd been away.
> None of my friends asked what the matter was –

> Everyone else had had a normal day.

Miracles Start like This

Unlikely though it is
That you remember, let alone adore me,
Miracles start like this –
God, or yourself, or Jim
May fix it for me.

It's the impossibility
That makes recovered sight miraculous
And the same mystery
That unblinds eyes
Could do some work for us.

Perhaps a need like mine
For you would be considered too small-scale
To attract much divine
Concern, in which case
This appeal may fail.

I've heard of people walking into flames
And coming out unhurt. Though I hold tight to
Faith, I would like some names
As well, of lesser saviours
I could write to.

Nostalgia

At playgroup I was fond of chasing boys
And pulling hair, and breaking people's toys.
My teachers said that I was a deranged
And selfish child. What makes you think I've changed?

At school it was a matter of survival;
You flattened, or were flattened by, your rival.
Normal procedure was to swear and spit
At enemies. I made the most of it.

At sixth form college, fights were strictly banned.
Hate was forced underground. We schemed and planned
Behind each other's backs, and realised
That spite was more effective when disguised.

I've ended up at university
Where both aggression and hypocrisy
Are seen as qualities to be eschewed.
It's wrong to punch, spread rumours or be rude,

Or so I'm told. True, there is much less grief
When everyone behaves, but the relief
Of striking back has gone, as have the joys
Of pulling hair and breaking people's toys.

Two Love Poems

POEM FOR A VALENTINE CARD

You won't find any hints
Enclosed, no cryptic clues, no fingerprints,

Nothing about the gender,
Background or occupation of the sender.

Anonymous, unseen –
You're dealing with the all-time king or queen

Of undercover loves.
The author of this valentine wore gloves.

RED MIST

You could wear different shoes,
Lose all the worthwhile things you have to lose;

You could go mad and howl
From a high tree through darkness, like an owl –

No part of me would change
However sick you were, however strange.

Your future, near and distant,
Is safe, as long as I remain consistent.

If, one day, you commit
A crime, I'll burn all evidence of it.

When it arrives, my doom
Will be a red mist entering the room.

Early Bird Blues

I am the early bird.
I have worn out my shoes
Simply because I heard
First come was first to choose.
One of my talents is avoiding queues.

I never ask how long
I shall be made to wait.
I have done nothing wrong.
I don't exaggerate.
To state the obvious, I'm never late.

Why has the queue not grown?
Nobody hears me speak.
I stand here all alone
Which makes me look unique
But even so, the worm avoids my beak.

What do the others know?
Have I been told a lie?
Why don't I turn and go?
I still know how to fly,
But, damn, I want that worm. I don't know why.

Your Street Again

'Guess who I saw last night?' was all she said.
That, and the answer (you), was all it took,
And now I'm leafing through my A-Z
To find your street again. I had to look

Four years ago, and memorise the way:
Palatine, Central, Burton – halfway there.
I don't intend to visit you today
As I did then, and so I shouldn't care

Which road comes after which and where they lead.
I do, though. I repeat them name by name.
My house is here and yours is there. I need
To prove the space between them stays the same.

Three Short Poems

A SOUL

And if I have a soul my soul is green
And if it sings it doesn't sing to me
And if it loves it loves externally
Both what it has and what it hasn't seen

And if it's green it may as well be high
And if ambition doesn't give it height
And if it only rises with a fight
Against itself and not against the sky

If all the force it uses leaves me free
This proves it not just definite but right

CATEGORIES

Some things resist division into parts:
The ventricles and atria of hearts –
The one is at a loss without the other.
The dead son slowly kills the living mother.

The dumbest mouths are those that miss their tongues.
The coldest air is far away from lungs.
Freedom is not what separation brings.
One person takes the bird and one the wings.

Each of us joins a different category
And what is in between ought not to be.

She knew a man who didn't quite recover
She owns a villa in the France of Spain
Your terraced husband has a penthouse lover
There's a come-uppance cruising down the lane

She hopes your terrace doesn't quite recover
She's confident her clothes cost more than yours
She introduced your husband to his lover
There's a come-uppance banging at the doors

She's feeling fragile just before the scene
There's a come-uppance in the fax machine

The Trouble with Keeping in Touch

In case you've ever asked yourself how long
A girl can sit and chew a ball-point pen,
Put down some words and then decide they're wrong
And cross the whole lot out and start again;

In case you've wondered how the record stands,
Take it from me (I know because I hold it) –
It's infinite; it constantly expands.
The truth can change just when you think you've told it.

Whatever may have happened to us both
Since I last smiled and waved and said goodnight to you,
Our lives continue growing, and the growth
Makes it impossible for me to write to you.

Ghazal

Imagine that a man who never writes
Walks on the planet Mars in cricket whites

Looking for signs of life which isn't there.
He walks through hot red days and dark red nights

Across a surface which is rough and bare.
He feels confused; he's come to see the sights

But there are none, and nobody to share
His empty mouth, his sudden fear of heights.

Nine of his cigarettes are going spare.
The tenth is for himself, and that he lights.

Something's familiar now. He starts to swear.
He stumbles through bizarre, one-sided fights.

Meanwhile you're stuck on Earth without the fare.
In any case, there are no scheduled flights.

And all the love you send is lost in air,
And all your words stick in the sky like kites.

Superstitions

I refuse to share my superstitions with anyone.
You can keep shoes off the table, walk around ladders,
Throw spilt salt over your shoulder, salute single magpies –
My behaviour, although insane, is at least original.

I look out of windows but never look into them.
I guard against colds with a fake Scandinavian accent
And I know I will have good luck when my path is crossed
Not by a black cat, but by a Chinese man called Norman.

This has happened twice in my life (same Norman both times).
Long fingernails are a bad omen. When I last grew mine
I found some unexplained underwear in my laundry bag
And was followed home by a man with a bushy moustache.

I'm telling the truth. I would never lie on a Friday.
This is not a superstition but what I was taught
By my mother, who used to say if you lose your cat
Give a hedgehog a saucer of milk and hope for the best.

The Usherette

When no-one tore my ticket up or said
No smoking – any seats except the red
I realised the usherette was dead.

A tray of ice-creams dangled at her side.
Her eyes were open and her hair was tied
Up at the back, just like before she died.

I gathered, from the coldness of her skin,
Death had occurred during the Gordon's Gin
Advertisement. Latecomers, trailing in,

Deposited their tickets in her palm
As, one by one, they passed her stiff, white arm
Showing no sign of interest or alarm.

They took their seats. I crouched down in the aisle,
Next to the usherette. Her frozen smile
Wouldn't release my stare. After a while

I fell asleep. What happened next was weird –
When I woke up her corpse had disappeared.
Nobody would believe me now, I feared.

After the film I waited by the door
Trying to memorise each face I saw
And then I left, since I could do no more.

Love Me Slender

LOVELY LESLEY LOST SIX STONE AND WON HER MAN

(*headline from the* Sun, *30 June 1993*)

You have to be size ten to get a bloke.
You must be slim, petite, and never podgy.
Since Stout is out you're left with Diet Coke
And other things that taste extremely dodgy.

You must be thin. Don't make me say it twice.
Size ten, or even twelve, but never fatter.
You may, in other ways, be very nice
But if you're overweight it doesn't matter.

You have to shed the pounds. It's such a drag.
You can't rely on brains or sense of humour.
It isn't true that many men will shag
Virtually anyone – that's just a rumour.

You need a model's figure, skin and bone,
Straight up and down without a single curve,
Unless you want to end up on your own,
Which, frankly, would be just what you deserve.

Morning Has Broken

The shark in *Jaws* was a lovable household pet.
Butch Cassidy and Sundance didn't die.
Scarlett and Rhett
did not split up. They gave it another try.

And you're a good egg, safe bet,
real brick. You're an honest guy.

The encounter was not so brief.
The bodies were never snatched.
Clyde Barrow wasn't a thief.

You're available, unattached –
no partner to give you grief.
We are well-matched.

Bergman and Bogart got back together
after the end of *Casablanca*.

I'm not at the end of my tether
and you're not a wanker.

As for last night,
neither my feelings nor my drinks were mixed
and it looks the same in the light.
Morning is fixed.

Skipping Rhyme for Graduates

I've got the motive.
I've got the stamina.
I'm going to kill
The external examiner.

Let crows and vultures
Pick at the carcass
After I've murdered
The stingiest of markers.

Bring out the bin-bags.
Bring out the spades.
Bring down the evil sod
Who brings down the grades.

Give me an alibi.
Give me a gun.
Wanted a first
But I got a two-one.

Just missed a first
By a fragment of a fraction.
Justice is called for,
Justice and action.

What a bloody miser!
What a bloody crook!
Won't mark another paper.
Won't write another book.

Won't see his bloody name
In another bloody journal.
Bye-bye, examiner.
Bye-bye, external.

Mountains out of Small Hills

Dogs are objecting to the word dogmatic,
the use of certain phrases – barking mad,
dog in the manger. Equally emphatic
are other species. Rats and snakes have had

enough of being symbols of deceit
and treachery. They say there's no excuse,
and there are fish protesting on the street
at being linked with alcohol abuse.

You couldn't taunt a coward nowadays
with 'scaredy-cat' or 'chicken'. Cock-and-bull
stories have been renamed. Nobody says
'God, she's a cow!' Nobody pulls the wool

over another person's eyes – the lambs
have seen to that. Nobody rabbits on.
Nor has there been a ramraid since the rams
petitioned parliament. We do not swan

around, get goosebumps; nothing gets our goat.
No cricket player ever scores a duck.
Once we were free with what we said and wrote.
Now we make do with swear-words. Bollocks. Fuck.

Reconstruction

Most of the witnesses were pissed.
The room is as it was before.
They do their best, but they persist
In seeing only what they saw
And missing what they've always missed.

They close their eyes. They walk around
But nothing seems to spring to mind.
How will they know when they have found
Whatever they're supposed to find?
Is it a smell? Is it a sound?

They do not know and cannot guess
What might be meant by evidence.
Since none of them would dare confess
Their presence here makes little sense,
But they are happy, more or less,

With things exactly as they are.
The first impression is the last.
If there is truth it lies too far
Away for them to reach. The past
Is like a disappearing star.

The Hero and the Girl Next Door

This story has at least one side.
The source is quite reliable.
The hero did his best. He tried,
But it was not a viable
Prospect, and so he burned his boats,
He cut his losses, changed his mind,
Dry-cleaned his most attractive coats
And left the girl next door behind.

His Christmas list had shed a name.
The girl next door had shed some tears,
But she was utterly to blame,
Had been, in fact, for several years.
Rewind. The lady vanishes.
Press stop, fast forward, then eject.
And what a silly girl she is.
And does she honestly expect...

So this is provocation, then,
And this is what they call just cause
And this is how you see it when
The hero is a friend of yours.
Another soldier saves his skin.
Another wrinkle ironed out.
You bet. You roll the dice. You win.
There is no reasonable doubt.

An Aerial View

Flight 608. The woman to my right
Has hardly touched the meal Air France provided.
She prods it with her fork as though she might,
Probably won't, but hasn't quite decided.

She eyes my empty tray with vague distaste –
I ate it all, and we were given loads.
She's proud of her restraint, her slender waist.
Neither will help her if the plane explodes.

She's frowning at my bottle of champagne,
Perhaps because it's only 8 a.m.,
But I don't care. When I am on a plane
My motto is 'enjoy myself – stuff them'.

Long-face can stick to water all the way,
That's up to her. I don't intend to slum it.
I'm pissed. She never drinks before midday.
Irrelevant distinction, if we plummet.

Last chance, perhaps, for grub and heavy drinking.
One shouldn't miss it. Here's what I advise:
Light up a fag, and concentrate on thinking
An aeroplane is just a pub that flies.

Absence Makes the Heart Grow Henry

Ann was the love of Colin's life
Until the day he went to meet her.
Later she became his wife
But absence makes the heart grow Peter.

Jack was obsessed with Debbie's writing.
Then one day he caught the train
And found the woman less exciting.
Absence makes the heart grow Jane.

I love you when you're not around.
If we come face to face again we
Stand to lose by being found,
For absence makes the heart grow Henry.

The Only Point is Decimal

Ninety per cent of places are not worth going.
Ninety per cent of jobs are not worth doing.
Ninety per cent of men are not worth knowing.
Ninety per cent of women are not worth screwing.

An attitude like yours must take some practice.
Part apathetic, mostly condescending,
Lukewarm then spiky, vichyssoise-cum-cactus,
That's you, my friend. Or are you just pretending?

Ninety per cent of books are not worth reading.
Ninety per cent of songs are not worth singing.
Ninety per cent of advice is not worth heeding.
Ninety per cent of numbers are not worth ringing.

Life passes by, but you are not impressed.
You'd rather be a lonely couch potato
Than compromise. There's no point getting dressed
For anyone less erudite than Plato.

Ninety per cent of chances are not worth taking.
Ninety per cent of corners are not worth turning.
Ninety per cent of hands are not worth shaking.
Ninety per cent of candles are not worth burning.

And all that I can think is what a shame.
What are the odds you'll wonder where I went?
The chances of you knowing why I came?
Point zero zero zero one per cent.

A Really Tacky Tourist Beach

Policemen wink and I relax.
I drive and drive but never see
A gift shop that's museum-free.
A sign beside the road says 'Snacks'.

The perfect morning for a race,
But there is no-one in my wake
And nobody to overtake.
I need another car to chase.

I drink and swim just like a fish.
One of these days I hope to reach
A really tacky tourist beach.
The traffic lights may grant my wish.

I have a stone called Sheriff John
And when I sing he sings along.
We do our favourite Beach Boys song.
Our skin is rough, our voices gone.

I pick a star and watch it rise;
Look left, look right. The mirror shows
A grinning mouth, a powdered nose
But nobody I recognise.

The Fairy Never Came to Get My Teeth

How can I help? I don't know when to clap
And when to throw a fit. It's not my day.
I've got a notebook sitting on my lap.
I can't get up until it goes away.

How do the neighbours know your bones are brittle?
I hear it from above you and beneath.
How's this for relevance: when I was little
The fairy never came to get my teeth.

I'm one of them, no longer one of us.
I haven't got the knack of self-expression
Like others have. I never make a fuss
Or jump the queue. I'm in the wrong profession.

The sawn-off shotgun in your biscuit tin,
The headless rodent in your Christmas stocking,
May drive me mad, but I will not barge in.
We're quaint round here. We still believe in knocking.

The smartest pupil in the haystack class
Pontificates all night: attack, defend...
Meanwhile there's no-one sweeping up the glass.
What you need most is not another friend,

Another eager face behind the door
To make you circulate a false address.
I keep away. Ask yourself who cares more.
A bigger crowd creates a bigger mess.

What do I think about an early grave?
Head-on collision with a wall or tree?
I think it's neither glamorous nor brave.
You need a louder audience than me.

You need a quiet night without a row.
You need a holiday. You need a fling.
(I hear my mother say *Be careful now*
And my reply: *I am becarefulling*.)

Leaving the house, dizzy from lack of lunch,
I pass two cold burritos in a trilby.
Each flippant story packs a careful punch.
It's not your day. I doubt it ever will be.

Fish Tony's Chips

Fish Tony's Chips. The marble god has eyes.
His handshake is a cupboard on the wall
In which a cabbage rots and changes size.

I constantly outgrow my overall.
Try something new. I hope you don't succeed.
Reserve that room for me or not at all.

We do not yet have all the words we need.
Check your thesaurus. Where's the word that means
To go out looking like a centipede?

To wear clean knickers under dirty jeans
And hold a bottle neck between your lips?
But what is happening behind the scenes?

The marble god has eyes. Fish Tony's Chips.

Bafield Load

Her desperation never showed.
For years she lived on Bafield Load

according to the envelope
that brought the final loss of hope.

From time to time she'd blink and shout:
There's nothing to be dead about,

but they'd already sprayed her grave
with cheap ex-boyfriend aftershave.

The Keyboard and the Mouse

I am myself and in my house
But if I had my way
I'd be the keyboard and the mouse
Under your hands all day.

I'd be the C prompt on the screen.
We could have had some fun
This morning, if I'd only been
Word Perfect 5.1.

I'd be your hard and floppy discs,
I'd be your laser jet,
Your ampersands and asterisks –
I'd be in Somerset

Rotating on your swivel chair.
The journey takes a while
But press return and I'll be there.
Do not delete this file.

The Safest Place

It's a hygienic lovers' tiff
That starts with if and only if
And tails off like a doctor's note.
How could you write the things you wrote,

Scaremongering? I'm sure we'll live.
Thank God my job's repetitive.
It keeps me calm – no hurt, no games.
I type a list of authors' names,

Relish the thought of getting bored.
I'm busy here. I can't afford
To fall apart or fall behind.
Everywhere else you're on my mind;

Work has become the safest place.
This catalogue, this database,
Proves, in a way, that life goes on.
Beaumont, Francis. Fletcher, John.

Triskaidekaphobia

Is it as easy as you make it sound?
You tell me not to cry on your account.
You didn't cry. I doubt you even frowned.
You sleep too easily when I'm around.
If I'm too much, are you the right amount?

This is about as open as I get.
Gram Parsons said love hurts and I agree
Although I haven't said I love you yet
And therefore have no right to be upset
Because you don't say anything to me.

We've really taken safety to extremes.
Reluctance makes us both insensitive.
They may come true, but would we call them dreams?
We're playground captains, calmly picking teams,
And even if there's nothing to forgive

You're hardly what a nice young girl expects,
If I can still describe myself as such –
Prostitutes, dogs and strange religious sects,
Your special drug and alcohol effects.
The message on your back reads please don't touch.

I see a threat in every paragraph,
Subject each letter to analysis.
I try and fail (you just can't get the staff)
To resurrect the flirt that made you laugh
But find her taking all your jokes amiss,

And all your views on dolls and boxing rings.
It's good to see your well-proportioned mind
Is on top form and full of different things.
Were you a child who didn't fall off swings
Unless there was a mattress close behind?

All right, I'm being totally unfair
But silence always makes me want to rant,
Like sneaking through the nothing to declare
Gate at the airport. I can hardly bear
Your morning walks. You're far too much like Kant.

A bit more truth over a few more days
And maybe panic would give way to sense.
Look at me now. I take a simple phrase
And blow it up in twelve pedantic ways,
Not out of spite, merely as self-defence.

This dot to dot is less than we deserve,
One of the many things I wish I'd said.
Until such time as I can find the nerve
I'll walk in ways that make the traffic swerve
And try to stop you getting out of bed.

When Will You Come and Identify my Body?

When will you come and identify my body?
It had better be soon or I might just take it amiss.
When will you come and identify my body?
Men basically do what they want, and I've only just realised this.

It was silly of me to drown in a shallow river,
Too small a gesture to impress the boys.
It was silly of me to drown in a shallow river.
They are either silent, or else they are making their football noise.

I would like to be buried with my shampoo and conditioner.
Once I was self-obsessed and even clean.
I would like to be buried with my shampoo and conditioner.
I'm aware that the cricket highlights start at eleven fifteen.

I have been deacidified and boxed.
You shouldn't have left me. You shouldn't have gone to the bar.
I have been deacidified and boxed.
You'll find me in pepper and pickle. You'll find me under the car

Or creeping up behind you with a trowel.
Are you a garlic crusher or a torch?
I'm creeping up behind you with a trowel.
You would never change. You would never redecorate the porch.

It's clear to me from the way you keep escaping
(Into halls, through doors) that you will never be ready.
It's clear, from me to the way you keep escaping.
When, though? When will you come? Will you come and identify
    my body?